MW00964750

Learning Tree
1 2 3

Trucks and Tractors

By Susan Baker

Illustrated by Mike Atkinson

CHERRYTREE BOOKS

Read this book and see if you can answer the questions at the end. Ask an adult or an older friend to tell you if your answers are right or to help you if you find the questions difficult. Often there is more than one answer to a question.

A Cherrytree Book

Designed and produced by
A S Publishing

First published 1990
by Cherrytree Press Ltd
a subsidiary of
The Chivers Company Ltd
Windsor Bridge Road
Bath, Avon BA2 3AX

Copyright © Cherrytree Press Ltd 1990

British Library Cataloguing in Publication Data
Baker, Susan
    Trucks and tractors.
    1. Motor vehicles
    I. Title II. Atkinson, Michael III. Series
    629.22

    ISBN 0-7451-5087-X

Printed and bound in Italy by L.E.G.O. s.p.a., Vicenza

tip-up
truck

tractor

Trucks and tractors move heavy loads.
They have powerful engines and big wheels.
We call most trucks lorries.
Never go near a moving truck.

Farmers use trucks to take food to market.
The animals go in trucks with open sides.

Trucks take goods from factories to the shops.
This lorry is carrying thousands of loaves of
bread.

This is a refrigerator truck.
It carries frozen food.

Tankers carry liquids. This is a petrol tanker.
It fills the underground tanks at the garage.

A car transporter carries several cars at once.
It brings new cars from the factory.

When you move house, your furniture is loaded
into a furniture van.

Some trucks have two parts.
They are called articulated trucks.
The front part is called the tractor.
It has a big engine underneath the driver's cab.

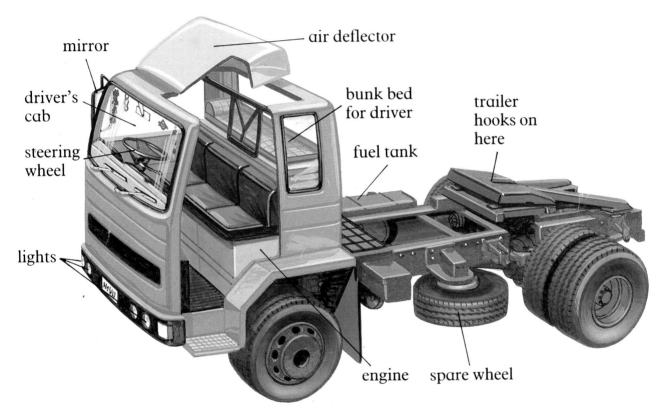

mirror

air deflector

driver's cab

bunk bed for driver

trailer hooks on here

steering wheel

fuel tank

lights

engine

spare wheel

Most articulated lorries are so big that the
drivers can sleep in them.

The front part pulls the back part.
The back part is called the trailer.
It carries the load.
It hooks on to the front part.

The two parts are connected but they can turn separately.
This makes it easier to turn corners and reverse into parking bays.
How does the driver see behind him when he is reversing?

break-down truck

Two trucks have had an accident.
A break-down truck tows away the small truck.
A bigger truck with a bigger crane will be
needed to right the big lorry.

The police hurry to help at an accident.
Ambulances take injured people to hospital.
Why is a fire engine often called to the scene?

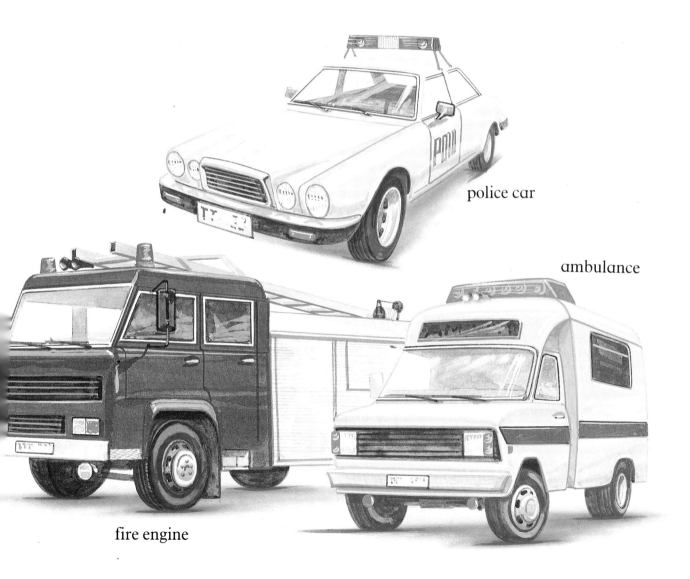

police car

ambulance

fire engine

A fork-lift truck picks up a load by sliding two forks between the layers of a pallet.
It lifts the load and moves it.
Then it puts it down and withdraws the forks.

fork-lift truck

tip-up truck or tipper

The back of a tipper lorry tips up.
The load slides out in a heap.

A grab-loader truck has its own grab for loading
and unloading pallets of bricks.

grab-loader
truck

earth
mover

This huge truck is an earth mover.
It shifts heavy loads on building sites.
It is an off-the-road truck.
It is too big and slow to travel far by road.

14

dumper
truck

This is an off-the-road dumper truck.
It carries a load in a bucket at the front.
It tips up to dump the load.

This little fork-lift truck is used indoors.
It is powered by an electric battery.

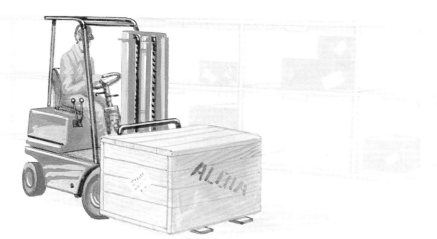

indoor
fork-lift
truck

Farmers use tractors on their farms to push or
pull tools and machines.
Tractors have very big wheels.
The tyres have thick rubber ridges.
They help it get a good grip on the land.

This tractor is pulling a plough.
The plough blades turn over the soil.
The tractor lifts the plough up to turn a corner.

This tractor is pulling a seed drill which plants seeds evenly.

This tractor is pushing a scraper at the front.

A caterpillar tractor has a long moving belt
around the wheels on each side.
The belt is made of metal tracks.
These grip the ground even better than tyres.

Caterpillar tractors can move on steep ground.
They can push or carry heavy loads.
This one is moving timber uphill.
It is called a bulldozer.

Caterpillar tractors are slow on roads.
This one is being moved on a low-loader truck.

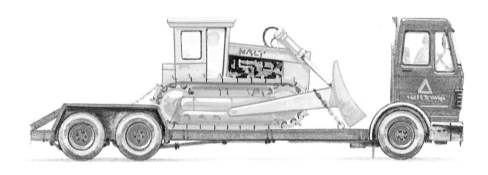

More about trucks and tractors

Trucks carry goods by road or work off the road carrying heavy loads. They bring us food, clothes, building materials and almost everything we use. They also take away our rubbish.

Lorries and trucks come in many sizes. Shops use delivery vans for small loads. Builders and farmers use pick-up trucks. They have a covered cab and an open back. Like cars, these lorries have petrol engines.

Large trucks, such as tractor-and-trailer trucks, usually have diesel engines. Diesel fuel is cheaper and goes further than petrol. Some small trucks like milk floats have electric engines.

In some countries, trucks tow two or three trailers, making a road train.

Most lorries carry less than two tonnes of material at a time. But some loaded lorries may weigh as much as 40 tonnes.

Off-the-road trucks may be even bigger. A giant tipper truck with six huge wheels may carry 100 tonnes.

Road trucks may have up to 20 wheels. There is a single pair at the front to make steering easy. Most of the back wheels are in double pairs to spread the weight of the load.

Long-distance truck drivers are allowed to drive for only a fixed number of hours. A machine called a tachograph in the cab measures the truck's speed and the time it spends on the road.

Truck drivers listen to the radio while they are driving. They also have radios they can speak on. They talk to other truck drivers and warn them of accidents or hold-ups.

Tractors have either petrol or diesel engines. The engine drives the wheels and also the machines that are attached to the tractor.

1

1 Look out for the trucks and lorries you have seen in this book. Be very careful. Do not go near trucks even when they are parked.

2 From a distance, count the wheels on a big truck.

3 Why do trucks and tractors have big engines?

4 Why do trucks carry a spare wheel?

5 Find out what this kind of truck is. What is its name?

2

6 If you are interested in trucks and tractors, keep a notebook about them. Write the answers to these questions in the notebook. Write other questions that occur to you in it. Make drawings of trucks and tractors that you see.

7 Look at the signs on the sides of trucks. Guess what is inside them.

8 Look out for these special trucks:
street-lighting truck
dustcart
cement mixer truck
milk tanker
milk float
fork-lift truck
Write down when and where you saw them.

9 Why do you think new cars are carried on a transporter?

10 What do you think the articulated truck on page 9 is carrying?

3

11 Why do pallets have a space between their two surfaces?

12 In which of these places would you be surprised to see an earth mover?
A mine, a quarry, a building site, a suburban garden.

13 Why are caterpillar tractors sometimes called crawlers?

14 A plough makes straight furrows in a field. Why does the tractor driver raise the plough when going round a corner?

15 Tractors have tools attached at the front or back. Which end should a plough go on? Which end should a scraper go on?

16 It is easy to count the wheels on one side of a passing truck. How can you work out how many wheels it has altogether?

17 Which feels heavier – a bag of sugar or a box of cornflakes? For which would you need a bigger truck – a thousand bags of sugar or a thousand packets of cornflakes?

18 Why do you hardly ever see caterpillar tractors on the road?

19 Why are some fuel pumps in garages labelled DERV? What do the letters stand for?

20 You may see the letters TIR on the back of some lorries. Find out what the letters stand for and what they mean.

21 Why do you think a bulldozer is so called?

22 Why do trucks that carry animals have open sides?

Index